HAMISH HENDERSON was born in 1919 in Blairgowrie in Perthshire, educated in Dulwich College and Cambridge University, and served in North Africa and Italy with the 51st Highland Division during the Second World War. As well as his poetry, Hamish was acclaimed for his songwriting and as a pioneer in the field of Scottish folksong. He died in March 2002.

Hamish Henderson

HAMISH
HENDERSON

ELEGIES FOR THE DEAD IN CYRENAICA

POLYGON

First published in 1948
by John Lehmann Ltd.
Revised editions published by EUSPB
in 1977 and Polygon in 1990.
This edition published in 2008
by Polygon, an imprint of
Birlinn Ltd
West Newington House
10 Newington Road
Edinburgh EH9 1QS

www.birlinn.co.uk

ISBN 978 1 84697 093 1

Copyright © Hamish Henderson 1948
This edition copyright © The estate of
Hamish Henderson 2008
1977 Introduction © Sorley MacLean 1977
2008 Introduction © Adrian Mitchell 2008

The right of Hamish Henderson to be
identified as the author of this work has
been asserted by him in accordance with
the Copyright, Designs and Patents
Act, 1988.

All rights reserved. No part of this
publication may be reproduced, stored, or
transmitted in any form, or by any means,
electronic, mechanical or photocopying,
recording or otherwise, without the express
written permission of the publisher.

British Library
Cataloguing-in-Publication Data
A catalogue record for this book is
available on request from the
British Library.

Typeset in Octavian by Dalrymple
Printed and bound in Britain
by CPI Antony Rowe, Chippenham,
Wiltshire.

CONTENTS

7 *Approaching the Elegies* Adrian Mitchell

11 *Introduction to the Second Edition*
   Sorley MacLean
15 *Preface to the First Edition*

17 Prologue

19 PART ONE
21 First Elegy *End of a Campaign*
23 Second Elegy *Halfaya*
25 Third Elegy *Leaving the City*
27 Fourth Elegy *El Adem*
29 Fifth Elegy *Highland Jebel*

31 Interlude *Opening of an Offensive*

35 PART TWO
37 Sixth Elegy *Acroma*
39 Seventh Elegy *Seven Good Germans*
43 Eighth Elegy *Karnak*
47 Ninth Elegy *Fort Capuzzo*
49 Tenth Elegy *The Frontier*

53 Heroic Song for the Runners of Cyrene

56 *Notes*
63 *Acknowledgements*

APPROACHING THE ELEGIES

Take your time. If you don't already know the outline of the North African campaigns of World War Two, you should discover it.

Ideally you should read, both before and after the Elegies, the first volume of Timothy Neat's excellent biography of Hamish Henderson. This will give you an idea of the nature of an extraordinary and much-loved poet. If possible, listen to recordings of Hamish reading and singing his poetry, in his warm and gentle voice.

Now take up this copy of *Elegies for the Dead in Cyrenaica* by my friend, the world's friend, Hamish Henderson. Read the modest verses of his Prologue first:

> *Against the armour of the storm*
> *I'll hold my human barrier,*
> *Maintain my fragile irony.*

He keeps that promise – the Elegies form one of the great testaments to the persistence of humanity, even in Hell.

Some writers try to turn war into a mighty legend full of larger-than-life warriors performing amazing deeds and feats of endurance – and there are fragments of truth to be found in such work, buried in a desert of lies. Some try to turn war into a fable or a fairy story or even an evil joke – but with all their faults, they do not turn their backs on the obscene fact that wars are still fought.

Hamish Henderson writes about war as war. His protagonists are life-size or death-size. He can write about war as war because he was there, in the middle of the war. The first Elegy, 'End of a Campaign', is itself a great poem. It maps out the deadliness of the desert. It records, in a brief agony, the deaths. It mourns, like Wilfred Owen, the corpses of both sides. It flies us, in two sentences, from the battlefield to a kitchen in Scotland and back to North Africa. And it ends with a great determination to bear witness to the deaths of the innocent, without hatred or bitterness.

All of the Elegies are worth your while – but read them out loud to your friends and loved ones to understand them properly. The poems work best in company. Listen to the music of their long and often melancholy lines – sometimes like the pipes heard from a distance.

Although these are true elegies, they are not simply about the past. 'Acroma' is a deeply sad poem, but it looks forward to a time of reconciliation and healing.

The quietly named Interlude becomes a rallying cry to all humane men and women to work against all oppressors, liars, warmongers and tyrants. It is among the many poems of Hamish which would be cheered by Blake and Burns, his brothers.

> So the book begins with five Elegies,
> like five different standing stones,
> stones of subtly different colours
> and shapes and attitudes.
>
> Then an interlude calls us to mental strife against
> international capitalism if you want the plain truth.
>
> Then five more Elegies all different
> like five more standing stones,
> stones of subtly different colours
> and shades and attitudes.

And finally a Heroic Song
which ends with two protagonists
wrestling, locked in each other's arms
and falling down a cataract
like Holmes and Moriarty
at the Reichenbach Falls.

The Elegies are not only poems about one of the most crucial battles of the twentieth century, with insights into modern history of Europe and Scotland and North Africa. They are a necklace of many-coloured stones to be worn and displayed to remind us what we have lost.

Hamish saw the whole poem as 'a remembrancer' in the hope that it would help create a free Scotland and a better world. It is worth your study, your enjoyment and a place in your heart.

ADRIAN MITCHELL, 2008

Adrian Mitchell was born near Hampstead Heath, London, in 1932. He is an Anglo-Scottish pacifist poet, performer, playwright and novelist for both children and adults. When appearing at the Edinburgh Festival he aloway dropped in on Sandy Bell's to enjoy the company, poems and stories of Hamish Henderson, who always greeted him with a large dram and a even larger smile.

INTRODUCTION TO
THE SECOND EDITION

Hamish Henderson's *Elegies for the Dead in Cyrenaica* first appeared in book form in 1948, but some of the Elegies were written as early as March 1943, and some existed in fragmentary form as early as the autumn of 1942, when Hamish was first in action, at the Battle of Alam Halfa. This began on 31 August 1942, that is, nearly two months before he shared in the first Desert actions of the Highland Division, at Alamein, on 23 October 1942. The Interlude, between the Fifth and Sixth Elegies, commemorates the tremendous barrage of that October night. The Elegies gained the Somerset Maugham Award and earned the praise of men like Day Lewis, E. P. Thompson and Giles Romilly, and one at least of the Desert's acknowledged bravest of the brave, Lorne MacLaine Campbell, VC. Afterwards, Henderson himself became a name among others of the bravest of the brave, Italian partisans. The book is thus the work of a man concerned not only with contemplating and recording a momentous piece of the world's history, but also with changing the world, even if it sees the war of 1939–45 not so much as action to change the world for the better but to prevent its change for the worse. The poet is a human being and 'negative capability' is only one of the qualities he may have, and even within 'negative capability' itself there is the implicit 'propaganda' of the choice. It is right that the 'Heroic Song for the Runners of Cyrene' should follow the ten Elegies, for even the 'innocence of the dead' does not reproach the necessary choice.

I did not know the Desert itself as extensively as Henderson did for I was never further west in it than the Gazala-

Bir Hacheim line, but the geographical setting of the book is ostensibly from Acroma in the west to Alexandria in the east. What I remembered of it in 1949, when I first read the Elegies, and what I still remember of it, responds sharply to the impact of the physical and psycho-physical 'feel' of it in the poems. For example, the psycho-geographical impression of the Halfaya–Sollum area in the opening verse paragraph of the Second Elegy is as true to me as anything I have read in war poetry.

In general, I remember the Desert itself as less 'malevolent' and 'brutish' than Henderson's record, for it could be even benign on summer nights, when bombs, shells and bullets left it alone; but it was often 'malevolent' and 'brutish' although 'impartial', with its cold on winter nights, its sandstorms and occasional Khamsins, which could cause such thirst that I have seen liquid margarine drunk when there was no water. It prolonged little cuts in 'Desert sores', and though the glitter and mirages of mid-day sometimes stopped the firing, they could also lead astray, as the sandstorms could too, and being led astray could sometimes mean death or captivity. It was a good battle-ground in that there was little of human achievement in it that could be destroyed except soldiers themselves and human means of destruction. The combatants were as if abstracted from a real world to fight on a remote moon-like terrain, and in general the only bitterness against the 'enemy' was when a soldier got news of deaths of his near and dear by civilian bombing at home. Then, if a man went berserk and fired at Germans with their hands up, he was promptly reminded by his comrades that two could play at that game. It was not a bitter war, and for some time after the German attack on

Russia, British prisoners were treated very well and even allowed to escape to carry back propaganda about the folly of being in the Desert at all.

The Foreword to the 1948 publication is perceptive and true about the '"doppelgaenger effect" . . . enhanced by the deceptive distances and uncertain directions of the North African wasteland . . . this odd effect of mirage and looking-glass illusion persisted, and gradually became for me the symbol of our human civil war, in which the roles seem constantly to change and the objectives to shift and vary . . .'. Hence the conflict seemed rather to be between 'the dead, the innocent — that wronged proletariat of levelling death in which all the fallen are comrades — and ourselves, the living, who cannot hope to expiate our survival but by "spanning history's apollyon chasm"'. The spanning of the chasm is symbolically adumbrated in the 'Heroic Song for the Runners of Cyrene', but it is fitful and muted in the Elegies, and rightly so, although there are dramatically true outbursts against the Fascists and Nazis, as in the conclusion of the Interlude and, more ambivalently, in the Ninth Elegy. The dominant tone is, however, the 'pity of it'.

The Sixth Elegy is sub-titled Acroma, on the Bir-Hacheim-Gazala line. Not by any means the best of Elegies, it is however true and significant in its sermopedestrian reportage of the under-statements of staff conferences changing poignantly to the 'criss-crossed enclosures' of the dead, which evoke only 'words of whole love'; and there are in it, and in the Seventh Elegy, poignant jabs such as that about the young German swaddy who 'had written three verses in appeal against his sentence Which soften for an hour the anger of Lenin'.

I have said that the Sixth is not the best of the Elegies, but that is only a relative verdict. It is a most impressive poem.

The Eighth Elegy sets the 'profound death-longing' emphasised in Karnak against the human realities of the Desert war enshrined in the plebeian language of the Ninth, back from Acroma to Fort Capuzzo, and the Tenth nobly juxtaposes the observations of a post-war air-line passenger over the frontiers of Egypt and Cyrenaica and the poignant memories and observations of a survivor of the war thinking of the war dead, and unable to 'fly from their scorn, but they close all the passes; their sleep's our unrest, we lie bound in their inferno —'.

The Elegies have their complexities: juxtapositions of soldier's talk, sometimes unthinking, violent but natural outbursts of men much under fire and propaganda, and the calmer thoughts of even the same men in the lulls of warfare in memorable and often noble language. Even the back and forward geographical movements of the poems seem the natural expression of the geographical fluctuations of the Desert War; but it is not such complexities of deliberate or intuitive post-Eliotian technique that make the book outstanding. To me its dominant quality is the fusion of its very particular Desert sensuousness with the particular and universal truth of its statement about the dead, reactions and actions of men under the stress of fast-moving war in such places as the North African Desert, and notably of the feelings of the survivor about the dead who have expiated their share of responsibility for war.

SORLEY MACLEAN, 1977

PREFACE TO THE FIRST EDITION

These Elegies and the Heroic Song in which they culminate were written between March 1943 and December 1947 in North Africa, in Italy and in Scotland. Four of them already existed in fragmentary form in the Autumn of 1942.

It was the remark of a captured German officer which first suggested to me the theme of these poems. He had said: 'Africa changes everything. In reality we are allies, and the desert is our common enemy.'

The troops confronting each other in Libya were relatively small in numbers. In the early stages of the desert war they were to a large extent forced to live off each other. Motor transport, equipment of all kinds and even armoured fighting vehicles changed hands frequently. The result was a curious 'doppelgaenger' effect, and it is this, enhanced by the deceptive distances and uncertain directions of the North African wasteland, which I have tried to capture in some of the poems.

After the African campaign had ended, the memory of this odd effect of mirage and looking-glass illusion persisted, and gradually became for me a symbol of our human civil war, in which the roles seem constantly to change and the objectives to shift and vary. It suggested too a complete reversal of the alignments and alliances which we had come to accept as inevitable. The conflict seemed rather to be between 'the dead, the innocent' — that eternally wronged proletariat of levelling death in which all the fallen are comrades — and ourselves, the living, who cannot hope to expiate our survival but by 'spanning history's apollyon chasm'.

Above all, perhaps, the doppelgaenger symbol allowed me to re-state in dialectical terms the endless problem of how to safeguard our human house. It is not enough surely to repeat or to re-phrase the words of the great makar –

> *No state in Erd here standis sicker;*
> *As with the wynd wavis the wicker*
> *So wannis this world's vanitie.*

As the processes of history become clearer, one must, in spite of all disorientation and despair, have the courage to be consequent and to acclaim the 'runners' who have not flinched before their ineluctable exploit.

In the first part of the cycle, echoes of earlier warfare and half-forgotten acts of injustice are heard, confusing and troubling the 'sleepers'. It is true that such moments are intended to convey a universal predicament; yet I was thinking especially of the Highland soldiers, conscripts of a fast vanishing race, on whom the dreadful memory of the clearances rests, and for whom there is little left to sustain them in the high places of the field but the heroic tradition of *gaisge* (valour).

Before leaving Italy I discussed the ideas I have outlined above with one of my Roman friends, the Editor of a literary quarterly. His comment was: 'Surely, having been so much in the midst of things, you must find it very difficult to be impartial.'

He was, I suppose, quite right. It certainly *is* terribly difficult, if one has been (to use his phrase) in the midst of things. However, as I gradually get the hang of how people form their opinions, I begin to feel that it is next to impossible if one has not.

HAMISH HENDERSON, 1948

Prologue
(for John Speirs)

Obliterating face and hands
The dumb-bell guns of violence
Show up our godhead for a sham.
Against the armour of the storm
I'll hold my human barrier,
Maintain my fragile irony.

I've walked this brazen clanging path
In flesh's brittle arrogance
To chance the simple hazard, death.
Regretting only this, my rash
Ambitious wish in verse to write
A true and valued testament.

Let my words knit what now we lack
The demon and the heritage
And fancy strapped to logic's rock.
A chastened wantonness, a bit
That sets on song a discipline,
A sensuous austerity.

PART ONE

Alles geben die Götter, die unendlichen,
Ihren Lieblingen ganz.
Alle Freuden, die unendlichen,
Alle Schmerzen, die unendlichen, ganz.

The gods, the unending, give all things
without stint to their beloved:
all pleasures, the unending,
and all pains, the unending, without stint.

GOETHE

FIRST ELEGY

End of a Campaign

There are many dead in the brutish desert,
> who lie uneasy
among the scrub in this landscape of half-wit
stunted ill-will. For the dead land is insatiate
and necrophilous. The sand is blowing about still.
Many who for various reasons, or because
> of mere unanswerable compulsion, came here
and fought among the clutching gravestones,
> shivered and sweated,
cried out, suffered thirst, were stoically silent, cursed
the spittering machine-guns, were homesick for Europe
and fast embedded in quicksand of Africa
> agonized and died.
And sleep now. Sleep here the sleep of the dust.

There were our own, there were the others.
Their deaths were like their lives, human and animal.
There were no gods and precious few heroes.
What they regretted when they died had nothing to do with
> race and leader, realm indivisible,
laboured Augustan speeches or vague imperial heritage.
(They saw through that guff before the axe fell.)
> Their longing turned to
the lost world glimpsed in the memory of letters:
an evening at the pictures in the friendly dark,
two knowing conspirators smiling and whispering secrets;
> or else
a family gathering in the homely kitchen

with Mum so proud of her boys in uniform:
> their thoughts trembled

between moments of estrangement, and ecstatic moments
of reconciliation: and their desire
crucified itself against the unutterable shadow of someone
whose photo was in their wallets.
Then death made his incision.

There were our own, there were the others.
Therefore, minding the great word of Glencoe's
son, that we should not disfigure ourselves
with villainy of hatred; and seeing that all
have gone down like curs into anonymous silence,
I will bear witness for I knew the others.
Seeing that littoral and interior are alike indifferent
and the birds are drawn again to our welcoming north
why should I not sing *them*, the dead, the innocent?

SECOND ELEGY

Halfaya
(For Luigi Castigliano)

At dawn, under the concise razor-edge
of the escarpment, the laager sleeps. No petrol fires yet
blow flame for brew-up. Up on the pass a sentry
inhales his Nazionale. Horse-shoe curve of the bay
grows visible beneath him. He smokes and yawns.
Ooo-augh,
         and the limitless
shabby lion-pelt of the desert completes and rounds
his limitless ennui.

At dawn, in the gathering impetus of day, the laager sleeps.
Some restless princes dream: first light denies them
the luxury of nothing. But others their mates more lucky
drown in the lightless grottoes. (Companionable death
has lent them his ease for a moment.)
         The dreamers remember
a departure like a migration. They recall a landscape
associated with warmth and veils and pantomime
but never focused exactly. The flopping curtain
reveals scene-shifters running with freshly painted
incongruous sets. Here childhood's prairie garden
looms like a pampas, where grown-ups stalk (gross outlaws)
on legs of tree trunk: recedes: and the strepitant jungle
dwindles to scruff of shrubs on a docile common,
all but real for a moment, then gone.
         The sleepers turn
gone but still no nothing laves them.

O misery, desire, desire, tautening cords of the bedrack!
Eros, in the teeth of Yahveh and his tight-lipped sect
confound the deniers of their youth! Let war lie wounded!

Eros, grant forgiveness and release
and return – against which they erect it,
the cairn of patience. *No dear, won't be long now
keep fingers crossed, chin up, keep smiling darling
be seeing you soon.*

On the horizon fires fluff now,
further than they seem.

       Sollum and Halfaya
a while yet before we leave you in quiet
and our needle swings north.

       The sleepers toss
and turn before waking: they feel through their blankets

the cold of the malevolent bomb-thumped desert,
impartial
hostile to both.

The laager is one.
Friends and enemies, haters and lovers
both sleep and dream.

THIRD ELEGY

Leaving the City

*Morning after. Get moving. Cheerio. Be seeing you
when this party's over. Right, driver, get weaving.*

The truck pulls out
along the corniche. We dismiss with the terseness
of a newsreel the casino and the column,
the scrofulous sellers of obscenity,
the garries, the girls and the preposterous skyline.

Leave them. And out past the stinking tanneries,
the maritime Greek cafes, the wogs and the nets
drying among seaweed. Through the periphery of the city
itching under flagrant sunshine. Faster. We are nearing
the stretch leading to the salt-lake Mareotis.
Sand now, and dust-choked fig-trees. This is the road
where convoys are ordered to act in case of ambush.
A straight run through now to the coastal sector.
One sudden thought wounds: it's a half-hour or over
since we saw the last skirt. And for a moment we regret
the women, and the harbour with a curve so perfect
it seems it was drawn with the mouseion's protractor.

Past red-rimmed eye of the salt-lake. So long then,
holy filth of the living. We are going to the familiar
filth of your negation, to rejoin the proletariat
of levelling death. Stripes are shed and ranks levelled
in death's proletariat. There the Colonel of Hussars,
the keen Sapper Subaltern with a first in economics

and the sergeant well known in international football
crouch with Jock and Jame in their holes like helots.
Distinctions become vain, and former privileges quite pointless
in that new situation. See our own and the opponents
advance, meet and merge: the commingled columns
lock, strain, disengage and join issue with the dust.

Do not regret
that we have still in history to suffer
or comrade that we are the agents
of a dialectic that can destroy us
but like a man prepared, like a brave man
bid farewell to the city, and quickly
move forward on the road leading west by the salt-lake.
Like a man for long prepared, like a brave man,
like to the man who was worthy of such a city
be glad that the case admits no other solution,
acknowledge with pride the clear imperative of action
and bid farewell to her, to Alexandria, whom you are losing.

And these, advancing from the direction of Sollum,
swaddies in tropical kit, lifted in familiar vehicles
are they mirage – ourselves out of a mirror?
No, they too, leaving the plateau of Marmarica
for the serpentine of the pass, they advancing towards us
along the coast road, are the others, the brothers
in death's proletariat, they are our victims and betrayers
advancing by the sea-shore to the same assignation.
We send them our greetings out of the mirror.

FOURTH ELEGY

El Adem

Sow cold wind of the desert. Embittered
reflections on discomfort and protracted absence.
Cold, and resentment stirred at this seeming
winter, most cruel reversal of seasons.
The weather clogs thought: we give way to griping
and malicious ill turns, or instinctive actions
appearing without rhyme or reason. The landsknechte
read mail, play scat, lie mute under greatcoats.
We know that our minds are as slack and rootless
as the tent-pegs driven into cracks of limestone,
and we feel the harm of inaction's erosion.
We're uneasy, knowing ourselves to be nomads,
impermanent guests on this bleak moon-surface
of dents and ridges, craters and depressions.
Yet they make us theirs: we know it, and abhor them,
vile three in one of the heretic desert,
sand rock and sky . . . And the sow wind, whipping
the face of a working (or a dying) unit
who shoulders his shovel with corpse obedience.

The sons of man
grow and go down in pain: they kneel for the load
and bow like brutes, in patience accepting the burden,
the pain fort and dour . . . Out of shuttered Europe
not even a shriek or a howl for its doomed children
is heard through the nihilist windvoice. Tomorrow's victors
survey with grief too profound for mere lamentation
their own approaching defeat: while even the defeated

await dry-eyed their ineluctable triumph.
Cages are crammed: on guard crouch the fearful oppressors
and wait for their judgment day.
       Therefore recollecting
the ice-bound paths, and now this gap in the mine-fields
through which (from one side or the other) all must pass
shall I not speak and condemn?

Or must it always
seem premature: the moment always at hand,
and never arriving, to use
our rebellious anger for breaking
the vicious fetters that bind us?

Endure, endure. There is as yet no solution
and no short cut, no escape and no remedy
but our human iron.
       And this Egypt teaches us
that mankind, put to the torment, can bear
on their breast the stone tomb of immolation
for millennia. The wind. We can build our cairn.

FIFTH ELEGY

Highland Jebel
(For John Lorne Campbell)

Was ist es, das an die alten seligen Küsten mich
fesselt, dass ich sie mehr liebe als mein eigenes Land?
HOELDERLIN

Our eyes, fatigued by the unsearchable desert's
moron monotony, lifted to the hills.

Strong-winged
our homing memory held us
on an unerring course: soared, leaving behind it
in an instant camp, coast-line and city,
sea, imbecile wasteland and the black sierras
for a well-known house.
         It found the treeless machair,
took in bay and snub headland, circled kirkyard and valley
and described once again our love's perfect circuit
till, flying to its own,
it dashed itself against the unresponsive windows.

So we waited
and lifted our eyes to
the hills, whence comes aid.

In our ears a murmur
of wind-borne battle. Herons stalk
over the blood-stained flats. Burning byres
come to my mind. Distance blurs
motive and aim. Dark moorland bleeding

for wrong or right.
*Sons of the hounds
come here and get flesh*. Search, bite!

In what deep antre
of death is there refuge
from this living rock?

Beyond the gate of the pass
are a high and low road: but neither
is the road back. No, laochain, they must lead us
in the hauteur of battle. Must array, enroll us
among listening cohorts. Where both vaunting and atonement
remain muffled for ever. The caverns will number
our momentary cries among the stounds and echoes
of this highland's millennial conflict.
Another falls for Hector.
                       Again there!
                                   Aye, in spite of
the houses lying cold, and the hatred that engendered
the vileness that you know, we'll keep our assignation
with the Grecian Gael. (And those others.) Then foregather
in a gorge of the cloudy jebel
older than Agamemnon.

Travelling light, and making the most of
the early coolness, we'll come before morning
to the raw uplands, and then by evening greet you
in the wilderness of you white corries, Kythairon.

INTERLUDE

Opening of an Offensive

(a) the waiting

Armour has foregathered, snuffling
through tourbillions of fine dust.
The crews don't speak much. They've had
last brew-up before battle. The tawny
deadland lies in a silence
not yet smashed by salvoes.
No sound reaches us
from the African constellations.
The low ridge too is quiet.
But no fear we're sleeping,
no need to remind us
that the nervous fingers of the searchlights
are nearly meeting and time is flickering
and this I think in a few minutes
while the whole power crouches for the spring.
x—20 in thirty seconds. Then begin

(b) the barrage

Let loose (rounds)
the exultant bounding hell-harrowing of sound.
Break the batteries. Confound
the damnable domination. Slake
the crashing breakers-húrled rúbble of the guns.
Dithering darkness, we'll wake you! Héll's bélls
blind you. Be broken, bleed
deathshead blackness!

      The thongs of the livid
firelights lick you
    jagg'd splinters rend you underground
we'll bomb you, doom you, tomb you into grave's mound

   (c) the Jocks

They move forward into no man's land, a vibrant sounding board.

   As they advance
the guns push further murderous music.
Is this all they will hear, this raucous apocalypse?
The spheres knocking in the night of Heaven?
The drummeling of overwhelming niagara?
No! For I can hear it! Or is it? . . . tell
me that I can hear it! Now — listen!

   Yes, hill and shieling
sea-loch and island, hear it, the yell
of your war-pipes, scaling sound's mountains
guns thunder drowning in their soaring swell!
— The barrage gulfs them: they're gulfed in the clumbering guns,
gulfed in gloom, gloom. Dumb in the blunderbuss black —
lost — gone in the anonymous cataract of noise.
Now again! The shrill war-song: it flaunts
aggression to the sullen desert. It mounts. Its scream
tops the valkyrie, tops the colossal
    artillery

Meaning that many
German Fascists will not be going home
meaning that many
will die, doomed in their false dream

We'll mak siccar!
Against the bashing cudgel
against the contemptuous triumphs of the big battalions
mak siccar against the monkish adepts
of total war against the oppressed oppressors
mak siccar against the leaching lies
against the worked out systems of sick perversion
mak siccar
         against the executioner
against the tyrannous myth and the real terror
mak siccar

PART TWO

'Na shuidhe marbh an 'Glaic a' Bhàis'
fo Dhruim Ruidhìseit,
gille òg 's a logan sìos m' a ghruaidh
's a thuar grìsionn.

Smaoinich mi air a' chòir 's an àgh,
a fhuair e bho Fhurair,
bhith tuiteam ann an raon an àir
gun éirigh tuilleadh . . .

Ge b'e a dheòin-san no a chàs,
a neo-chiontas no mhìorun,
cha do nochd e toileachadh 'na bhàs
fo Dhruim Ruidhìseit.

SOMHAIRLE MAC GILL-EAIN

Sitting dead in 'Death Valley'
below the Ruweisat Ridge,
a boy with his forelock down about his cheek
and his face slate-grey.

I thought of the right and joy
he had from his Fuehrer,
of falling in the field of slaughter
to rise no more . . .

Whatever his desire or mishap,
his innocence or malignance,
he showed no pleasure in his death
below the Ruweisat Ridge.

SORLEY MACLEAN

SIXTH ELEGY

Acroma

Planning and execution
recede: the preliminary inertia,
the expectation, the lull, the relaxing and the encounter's
suddenness recede, become history: thrusts, sieges and feints
that still blood maps with arrows
and left dead like refuse, these are the basis
of battle studies. And we're no better. The lying films
contain greater truth than most of our memories.

And the participants? — Staff Officers consider,
discuss and record their provisional verdicts.
These were go-getters, professional outflankers,
capable assault troops, or specialists in night warfare;
while those others had guts and lacked training, yet put up
a decent enough show at Himeimat or Munassib.
Occasionally there are doubts, dispute becomes acrimonious,
the case is not proven, judgment must be deferred.
On one point however there is unanimity: their sacrifice
though hard and heroic was on the whole 'necessary'.
I too have acquiesced
in this evasion: that the unlucky
or the destined must inevitably fall
and be impaled on the basalt pinnacles of darkness.

Yet how can I shame them, saying that they
have died for us: that it was expedient
a generation should die for the people?

To justify them, what byways must I follow?
Into what inaccessible sierras
of naked acceptance, where mere reason cannot live,
where love shines like a glacier. Could I ever attain it?
Neither by dope of reportage, nor by anodyne of statistics
is *their* lot made easier: laughing couples at the tea-dance
ignore their memory, the memoirs almost slight them
and the queue forming up to see Rangers play Celtic
forms up without thought to those dead. — O, to right them
what requiem can I sing in the ears of the living?

No blah about their sacrifice: rather tears or reviling
of the time that took them, than an insult so outrageous.
All barriers are down: in the criss-crossed enclosures
where most lie now assembled in their aching solitude
those others lie too — who were also the sacrificed
of history's great rains, of the destructive transitions.
This one beach where high seas have disgorged them like flotsam
reveals in its nakedness their ultimate alliance.

So the words that I have looked for, and must go on looking for,
are worlds of whole love, which can slowly gain the power
to reconcile and heal. Other words would be pointless.

SEVENTH ELEGY

Seven Good Germans

*The track running between Mekili and Tmimi was at one time
a kind of no-man's-land. British patrolling was energetic, and there
were numerous brushes with German and Italian elements.
El Eleba lies about halfway along this track.*

          Of the swaddies
               who came to the desert with Rommel
there were few who had heard (or would hear) of El Eleba.
They recce'd,
          or acted as medical orderlies
or patched up their tanks in the camouflaged workshops
and never gave a thought to a place like El Eleba.

To get there you drive into the blue, take a bearing
and head for damn-all. Then you're there. And where are you?

— Still, of some few who did cross our path at El Eleba
there are seven who bide under their standing crosses.

The first a Lieutenant.
          When the medicos passed him
for service overseas, he had jotted in a note-book
*to the day and the hour   keep me steadfast   there is only
the decision and the will*
                      the rest has no importance

The second a Corporal.
>
>He had been in the Legion
and had got one more chance to redeem his lost honour.
What he said was
Listen here, I'm fed up with your griping —
If you want extra rations, go get 'em from Tommy!
You're green, that's your trouble. Dodge the column, pass the buck
and scrounge all you can — that's our law in the Legion.
You know Tommy's got 'em . . . He's got mineral waters,
and beer, and fresh fruit in that white crinkly paper
and God knows what all! Well, what's holding you back?
Are you windy or what?
>
>*Christ, you 'old Afrikaners'!*
If you're wanting the eats, go and get 'em from Tommy!

The third had been a farm-hand in the March of Silesia
and had come to the desert as fresh fodder for machine guns.
His dates are inscribed on the files, and on the crosspiece.

The fourth was a lance-jack.
>
>He had trusted in Adolf
while working as a chemist in the suburb of Spandau.
His loves were his 'cello, and the woman who had borne him
two daughters and a son. He had faith in the Endsieg.
THAT THE NEW REICH MAY LIVE prayed the flyleaf of his
>
>Bible.

The fifth a mechanic.
>
>All the honour and glory,
the siege of Tobruk and the conquest of Cairo
meant as much to that Boche as the Synod of Whitby.
Being wise to all this, he had one single headache,
which was, how to get back to his sweetheart (called Ilse).
— He had said

Can't the Tommy wake up and get weaving?
If he tried, he could put our whole Corps in the bag. May
God damn this Libya and both of its palm-trees!

The sixth was a Pole
                 – or to you, a Volksdeutscher –
who had put off his nation to serve in the Wehrmacht.
He siegheiled, and talked of 'the dirty Polacken',
and said what he'd do if let loose among Russkis.
His mates thought that, though 'just a polnischer
                               Schweinhund',
he was not a bad bloke.
                On the morning concerned
he was driving a truck with mail, petrol and rations.
The M.P. on duty shouted five words of warning.
He nodded
        laughed
               revved
                       and drove straight for El Eleba
not having quite got the chap's Styrian lingo.

The seventh a young swaddy.
                Riding cramped in a lorry
to death along the road which winds eastward to Halfaya
he had written three verses in appeal against his sentence
which soften for an hour the anger of Lenin.

                Seven poor bastards
                dead in African deadland
                (tawny tousled hair under the issue blanket)
                wie einst Lili
dead in African deadland

                             einst Lili Marlene

EIGHTH ELEGY

Karnak
Er lächelt über die ganze Welt hinaus

Surely it is a holiday
or a day of national thanksgiving. – Observe the King
as he offers up the spoils of Syria to Osiris.
No doubt he is acknowledging
the conclusion of some war to preserve civilization.

Insolence of this civilization,
to counterfeit with such assurance the eternal!

Yes, here among the shambles of Karnak
is Vollendung unknown to the restless Greeks.
Here, not in Elis and Olympia
are edle Einfalt und stille Grösse.
They bore many children
but their triumphal barque of civilization
was weighed down with a heavy ballast
of magnetic death.
There is the Schwerpunkt, not here,
there across the river that made it all possible
the dead were taken across death
(listen to the waves of the flowing symbol,
lisping death) were taken to temporary slumber
and were introduced with courtesy to Osiris
and the immortal macabre company

        But the envious desert
held at arm's length for millennia
had its own way at last —
        in the name of Mohammed
the nomads conquered:

        though not for the first time.
It had all happened before, as is the confounding way of history:
when the shepherd kings, Yaakeb and Yusuf,
heavy breathing with their hairy gutturals,
stood incredulously in the courts of Amun.
They looked down their noses at the phallic Min
and took up stones against impassive Osiris.
(Not of them hawk Horus, or the clerkish Thoth,
not of them the complacence on the lips of Pharaoh
not of them the capitals of lotus and papyrus.)

Those who go a-whoring after death
will assuredly find it. Will be sealed in, confined
to their waste palaces. And Karnak the temple
be 'stalls for the nomads'.

        Puff of dust
on the blurred horizon means the imminent approach
of the solution, of subjection-deliverance.
These horsemen are merciful, they bring
the craved annihilation.
These are 'my servants, the Assyrians',
        these the necessary antithesis,
these the standard-bearers of the superb blasphemy,
felling gods, levelling cities,
death-life grappling with life-death, severing
the umbilical cord of history.

These are the trampling migrations of peoples,
the horsemen of Amr, the 'barbarians' of Cavafy
and Rommel before the gates of Alexandria.

But still, in utter silence, from bas-relief and painted tomb
this civilization asserts
its stylised timeless effrontery.
Synthesis is implicit
in Rilke's single column, (die *eine*)
denying fate, the stone mask of Vollendung.
(Deaf to tarbushed dragoman
who deep-throatedly extols it.)

Yes, pinned with paint to walls, deep in stone carved, they cannot
resent the usurper. They fix and hold motionless
a protracted moment of time, a transitory eon.

The sun-boat travels through the hours of darkness
and Ra mounts heavenwards his chosen path.

What will happen during this day?
       Will the King's Vizier
find time to be present at his public function?
Will silly girls fight among the stooks: will a sailor
be beaten for insubordination?

Is the harvest home yet: will stewards be computing
in the household office the extent of their surplus?
Will patient labourers work the shadouf?
Is fruit on the branch: and will ripe pomegranates
be shipped down to Thebes? Will rough Greeks land on Pharos?
Will prisoners of war drive the shaft for a tomb?
Is scaffolding up? Will the subsidized craftsmen

work diligently still on their couple of colossi,
all masters of the chisel, its calculated cutting?
Are Bedouin herds moving up from the South?

Will it be a feast-day: will the smooth priests
in bell-bottomed robes process between the sphinxes?
Detesters of the disk, possessors of the mystery,
shrewd guardians of the vested interests of Amun!
Where will the King be? Out boating for his pleasure;
while his boat shears through the Nile reeds
he aims at wild fowl with a boomerang —
Can he be sure of bringing home a bag?
         No doubt the court
will see to it, being solicitous.

In the evening he will return to Thebes, in his state
chariot, with the music of many instruments.
To his fellaheen a vision of flower strewn godhead
the scourge and the crook, under the sycamore leaves of life

         of life
         o unheeding
         the long ambiguous shadow
         thrown on overweening temple
         by the Other, the recurrent
         the bearded
         the killer in the rhythmical tragedy
         the heir   the stranger

Welcome O Hussein
When you enter Karbala

NINTH ELEGY

Fort Capuzzo

*For there will come a day
when the Lord will say
— Close Order!*

One evening, breaking a jeep journey at Capuzzo
I noticed a soldier as he entered the cemetery
and stood looking at the grave of a fallen enemy.
Then I understood the meaning of the hard word 'pietas'

(a word unfamiliar to the newsreel commentator
as well as to the pimp, the informer and the traitor).

His thought was like this. — Here's another 'Good Jerry'!
Poor mucker. Just eighteen. Must be hard-up for man-power.
Or else he volunteered, silly bastard. That's the fatal
the — fatal — mistake. Never volunteer for nothing.
I wonder how he died? Just as well it was him, though,
and not one of our chaps . . . Yes, the only good Jerry,
as they say, is your sort, chum.
        Cheerio, you poor bastard.
Don't be late on parade when the Lord calls 'Close Order'.
Keep waiting for the angels. Keep listening for Reveille.

TENTH ELEGY

The Frontier

One must die because one knows them, die
of their smile's ineffable blossom, die
of their light hands

But dust blowing round them
has stopped up their ears
                       o for ever
not sleeping but dead

The airliner's passengers,
crossing without effort the confines
of wired-off Libya, remember
little, regret less. If they idly
inspect from their windows the ennui
of limestone desert
         – and beneath them
their skimming shadow –
         they'll be certain
they've seen it, they've seen all

(Seen all, maybe, including
the lunar qattaras, the wadis like family trees,
the frontier passes with their toyshop spirals –
seen nothing, and seen all

And the scene yields them? Nothing)

Yet that coast-line

could yield much: there were recces and sorties,
drumfire and sieges. The outposts
lay here: there ran the supply route.
Forgotten.
        By that bend of Halfaya
the convoys used to stick, raw meat for the Jabos.

And here, the bay's horseshoe:
how nobly it clanged through laconic communiqués!

Still, how should this interest the airborne travellers,
being less real to them than the Trojan defence-works
and touching them as little as the Achaean strategies?
Useless to deny. The memorial's obsequious
falsehoods are irrelevant. It has little to arrest them,
survivors by accident
        that dried blood in the sangars.

So I turn aside in the benighted deadland
to perform a duty, noting an outlying
grave, or restoring a fallen cross-piece.
Remembrancer.
        And shall sing them who amnestied
escaped from the tumult to stumble across sand-dunes
and darken their waves in the sea, the deliverer.

Run, stumble and fall in their instant of agony
past burnt-out brennpunkt, along hangdog dannert.
Here gutted, or stuck through the throat like Buonconte,
or charred to grey ash, they are caught in one corral.
We fly from their scorn, but they close all the passes:
their sleep's our unrest, we lie bound in their inferno –
this alliance must be vaunted and affirmed, lest they condemn us!
Lean seedlings of lament spring like swordsmen around us;
the coronach scales white arêtes. Bitter keening
of women goes up by the solitary column.
Denounce and condemn! Either build for the living
love, patience and power to absolve these tormented,
or else choke in the folds of their black-edged vendetta!
Run, stumble and fall in our desert of failure,
impaled, unappeased. And inhabit that desert
of canyon and dream – till we carry to the living
blood, fire and red flambeaux of death's proletariat.
Take iron in your arms! At last, spanning this history's
apollyon chasm, proclaim them the reconciled.

HEROIC SONG FOR
THE RUNNERS OF CYRENE

(to Gregorio Prieto)

Without suffering and death one learns nothing.
We should not know the difference between the visions
of the intellect and the facts.
Only those ideas are acceptable that hold through
suffering and death . . .
Life is that which leaps.

DENIS SAURAT:
'Death and the Dreamer'

I

The runners who would challenge
            the rough bounds of the desert
and strip for the test
            on this barbarous arena
must have sinews like hounds
            and be cunning as jerboas.

Rooting crowds'll not hail them
            in boisterous circus
nor sleek fame crown their exploit
            with triumph and obelisk.
Sún beats their path
            down the hours of blank silence:
each knows that in the end
            he'll be lucky to have respite.

Freely they'll run
            to the chosen assignation;
ineluctable role,
            and they ready to accept it!
Going with élan of pride
            to the furious onset
they'll reclaim the dead land
            for their city of Cyrene.

Sún beats their path:
        this no course measured plainly
between markers on the beach,
        no event for the novice.
The gates open: are closed.
        And the track leads them forward
hard by salt-lake and standing stone
        blind as the cyclops.

While keeping the same pace
        neither slower nor faster
but as yet out of sight
        behind plateau and escarpment
is history the doppelgaenger
        running to meet them.

II

Stroke of the sun means the hour that's to lay them
is present once more on the dust-blurred horizon.
They start, and awake from their stupor of rhythm –
and think, as they catch glimpse of sea beyond watch-tower
they cannot be far from . . . a place they'd forgotten.

At last it is sure. O, they know that they'll never
be hesitant feet on the marches of darkness
or humped epigonoi, outliving the Fians.

No matter what hand stirs the dust, questions gently
with curious touch the grazed stones of the city
yon stroke of the sun vaunts their exploit for ever.

They quicken their pace. (And those others too.) Faster,
and livelier now than at jousts of the Toppo.
The goal is in sight. Simultaneous the onrush,
the clash close at hand, o incarnate dialectic!
The runners gain speed. As they hail their opponents
they can hear in the air the strum of loud arrows
which predestined sing to their point of intersection.
Blaze of harsh day stuns their human defiance;
steel beats their path with its pendulum brilliance.

Sun's thong is lifted. And history the other
emerges at last from the heat's trembling mirror.

III

           Their ruin upon them
they've entered the lip of the burning enclosure.
Each runs to achieve, without pause or evasion
           his instant of nothing

           they look for an opening
grip, grapple, jerk, sway
and fall locking like lovers

down the thunderous cataract of day.

Cyrene, 1942 – Carradale, Argyll, 1947

NOTES

The quotations used to introduce the two parts of the cycle need, perhaps, a word of elucidation. Goethe's quatrain was frequently included in small anthologies 'for the Front' carried by German soldiers in the field – and indeed its thought lies very near the mood of many of them. One might translate it as follows:

'The gods, the unending, give all things without stint to their beloved: all pleasures, the unending – and all paints, the unending, without stint.'

Set against this at the beginning of the second part is the sceptical ironic spirit of a Gaelic poet who fought in the desert and was wounded at El Alamein. Sorley MacLean translates his own poem thus:

'Sitting dead in "Death Valley" below the Ruweisat Ridge, a boy with his forelock down about his cheek and his face slate-grey. I thought of the right and joy he had from his Fuehrer, of falling in the field of slaughter to rise no more ... Whatever his desire or mishap, his innocence or malignance, he showed no pleasure in his death below the Ruweisat Ridge.'

THIRD ELEGY

The quotations in this poem are from 'The God Leaves Anthony' by the Greek Alexandrian poet, C. P. Cavafy (1868–1933).

In Cavafy's poem, Alexandria is a symbol of life itself.

FIFTH ELEGY

Laochain. Literally means 'little hero'. Familiar term of endearment for a young lad in Gaelic.

Another falls for Hector. Patroclus. – I was thinking also of the warcry of the Macleans who died in defence of their chief at Inverkeithing: *Fear eile airson Eachainn* (Another for Hector).

The Grecian Gael. Term occasionally used by the old bards for the Scots and Irish – Cf. the *Brosnachadh (Incitement to Rise)* addressed to Argyll before Flodden (Book of the Dean of Lismore).

INTERLUDE

Scaling sound's mountains.

> Wi' nocht but the cry o' the pipes can Earth
> Or these – or silence – meet.
> Hugh MacDiarmid.
> *Coronach for the End of the World.*

Mak siccar (Make sure). One of the famous phrases of mediaeval Scottish history.

After Bruce had stabbed the Red Comyn in Dumfries Kirk he was found outside the building by Lindsay and Kirkpatrick. Lindsay asked if Comyn were dead. Bruce replied that he didn't know.

'Aweel', said Kirkpatrick, 'I'll mak siccar'.

EIGHTH ELEGY

'This civilisation was filled, so great was its unshaken complacence on this earth, with a profound death-longing – it longed, dreamed, lusted, went a-whoring after death.

'Karnak, smashed, is the ironic image of Vollendung. The tombs in the Valley of the Kings are as good a sketch as man has made of "the eternal".

'I do not let myself be weighed down by the impassive timeless effrontery of this civilisation. I realise that all of us, from Hellenes to Gaelic outlanders of the western world are in a sense beside Thebes half-civilised clod-hoppers, hairy men with a lop-sided slant on time, half-baked hurried ignorant Yank tourists with a kink about progress mechanical or social.

'But you can have Luxor – it solves none of the problems, it doesn't even pose them. If we of the modern west devote a tenth of the time to life that Karnak devoted to death, we'll bring a tangible hope, even to the inhabitants of the Nile Valley.'

– *Extract from my notebook, 17 January 1943.*

The 'barbarians' of Cavafy. I was thinking of these lines in the poem 'Waiting for the Barbarians':

> 'And now what is to become of us without barbarians?
> These barbarians were a kind of solution.'

He aims at wild fowl with a boomerang. If any one doubts the authenticity of this reference, he should pay a visit to the tomb of Menna, which is among the nobles' tombs at Thebes.

NINTH ELEGY

The newsreel commentator. I was thinking particularly of one whose mike-side manner when referring to the area targets of Bomber Command or when delivering ignoble gibes at the expense of enemy front-line soldiers filled me (and plenty of others) with shame and fury.

TENTH ELEGY

Stuck through the throat like Buonconte.
      Dante, *Purg.* v. 88–129.

The episode of Buonconte was quoted to me by a Tuscan partisan in the hills north of Florence.

HEROIC SONG FOR THE RUNNERS OF CYRENE

Cyrene in this poem is for me a symbol of civilised humanity, of our 'human house'.

 The legend of the brothers Philaeni who competed against athletes from Cyrene suggested the symbol of the runners.

History the doppelgaenger

> Spectre of Albion! Warlike fiend!
> In clouds of blood and ruin rolled,
> I here reclaim thee as my own!
> My selfhood! Satan! Arm'd in gold.
>
> WILLIAM BLAKE

They cannot be far from. I had in my mind here a line which introduces the Skaggerrak motif in Reinhold Goering's play *Seeschlacht* (Sea Battle) – 'We cannot be far from the Skaggerrak'.

Seeschlacht, which appeared in 1917, was inspired by the Battle of Jutland fought the previous year – a battle known in German as the Skaggerrakschlacht. The opening scenes recreate with real skill the atmosphere of suspense before battle.

The play, incidentally, is well worth reading for its delineation of the German military mentality. Here are the dying words of a would-be mutineer who has after all distinguished himself in the fighting:

> I've done good work firing, eh? –
> And I'd have mutinied well, too, eh? –
> But the firing was nearer our hearts, eh? –
> Ay, it must have been nearer our hearts.

After the Fians
Oisein an déigh na Feinne (Ossian after the Fians) is a Gaelic proverbial expression. Ossian is reputed to have outlived his compeers, the Fingalian heroes.

Jousts of the Toppo
Dante, *Inferno*, xiii. 118–21. The fugitives in the Wood of the Suicides.

ACKNOWLEDGEMENTS

Acknowledgements are due to the editors of
the following reviews and anthologies, in
which these poems have variously appeared:
*Atlantic Anthology, New Road, New Writing
and Daylight, Our Time, Orientations* (Cairo),
*Penguin New Writing, Poetry Quarterly, Poetry
Scotland, The New Alliance, The Scots Review*
and *The Voice of Scotland.*
H.H.